I0117963

# Little Boy

# Paul Butterfield Jnr

**chipmunkapublishing**
the mental health publisher

Published by
Chipmunkapublishing
United Kingdom

**http://www.chipmunkapublishing.com**

ISBN    978-1-78382-040-5

Chipmunkapublishing gratefully acknowledge the support of Arts Council England.

Author Biography

Paul was born in the 12$^{th}$ of august 1989 and as a kid he wanted to venture in everything! It wasn't to Paul was 12 when he found his first love "skateboarding". When Paul was 15 he found martial arts for vengeance! Now he is a blackbelt under the guru of "Geoff Thompson" from that he had learned to be forgiving and peaceful! He then was inspired to be a personal development coach and he went to America and trained under "Bob Proctor and Paul Martinelli". But to Paul's surprise he was going to be hit with the biggest fight of his life "bi-polar disorder"! After a year with counsellors and psychiatrists Paul was diagnosed with manic depression! Paul didn't handle this so well for a couple of years and became self-destructive but there was one thing he wanted from he was 7 years old and that was to be a "writer"! Paul has kicked all aside and now is constructive and creative with his time through the written word and building himself up everyday from a broken man!

This is Paul's work over the last 5 years with living with bi-polar disorder! Venting his immense pain and devoted love through the written word of poetic form!

Enjoy!

# Little Boy

"gods a bastard, life's a nightmare or is it just me?"

A maggot to the apple

Eating me like a maggot to the apple
Why do you do such things to me?
It is not fair
My mind sensitive
Like a pin to the skin
An explosion from within
Out load
You still don't hear my echo
In this sphere!

Black shadow

Times were simpler back then, cast in the clean cloud of
sunshine, the lies, the deceit, knocked us back from the real,
it was fun and enjoyable.
Now I take the back alleys, with only me and my black
shadow, it's just not as much fun anymore.
But... I find snippets, as I scummage threw the rubbish of my
stoned chisel existence of death afar..!

But

Transparent gaze
Spearmint grace
I feel like you old man
A young man I am
Who's too old for these fresh boots?
Purple blossoms
How I grace your daze
Regretful repent of past
But…

Chaotic soul

Coal ignite… my stomach ache
Yet I still bear the death inside
Though my love hugs out in ecstasy
The monster still cry's and crawls all over me
In this bliss…
Chaos has crippled my soul
It still renders its beauty inside
Yet needs divide!
HEART… let go, let go
But obviously not…
For… what have I done wrong?
For taking a shot!

## Cofuffled

Blissful red... of this ignorance
Bug crawl my flesh
These hells will not steal my substance
My body treacle with water, as I mesh
Wearing thin as the nine
My love to hate
I watch out for that watchful sign
As her name maybe Kate
My energies are blocked
Who am I in this forge?
Two halves sealed, equals heart socked
An early rest in this morgue
But hell well risen, like a sippy cake
The boy in me cry's but would like to tout
God hear my cry for forgiveness, if I have forsaken you, now I
shall be awake
A lover's path, for all we can enjoy
A hater's barbed wire fortress, all will wail if followed
Cofuffled...!

Dark child of the night

I am the dark child of the night
A sky of obedience, yet so free
I dream away my happiness and love
Hoping that you will catch it in your net
I can crawl and ooze my wounds of darkness and anger
In this unlimited paced time
Night-time sky you are my friend
Though my enemy
But light… you are just too bright for my like!

Don't be a pansy... by the frying pan!

A year's divide
My stomach crushes into me
My imagination drifts helplessly
Secluded in mums coat
Disappearing into the wilderness
A simmering yellow glurp
Fuck off in anger I say

My heart on you now
Feeling wildly numb
Cry a clouded tear
The black dog erupts
Daddy's glove comes on, with the yellow fingered beast
I am a laughing crack

Meditating in silence and girth
I can't help to remember
You broke my already damaged heart and danced on my
foreskin

Remember us walking in that aqua mint air
A kiss in the middle of the night
With charges in our heats
I still carelessly love you
After all this time!

Evergreen

Afternoon rises
The sky set alight
A calm atmosphere blanket to cosy

Pink elephants and burnt down trees
Swims in the oceans of our minds

Electromagnetic waves curves this room
This call is waiting…
You are not ready yet

Two whites, with two canes
One black and a tobacco frosted cake

Let the multi-coloured flowers and purple bees
Shine and sail on our journey

Until they come back to haunt us
Out from the evergreen door!

## Existence

Living or existing? In the mind of imagination, theory only?
Music of the culture, dancing like the lights of a Christmas
tree on rotation.
Then those, music of the underground of truth, dancing like
the inner workings of a battery!
Smooth the fag, of the early bird chirping.
Sky twinkles and shine, awake of the manic of expression.
Sleeps of the chatters of coffees and work the hours of day.
The eyed triangle sets upon you, my existing brother and
sisters, of the book of life and wisdom of life, meant to be
lived, of purity and consistence!
The standards of block, in speech, preach of how, why, when
and where? But none of us, numbers of tagged and
calculators of not, have the answers of right.
But the wrong shall always be justified in the brown blanket of
mystery, KARMA, theory only?
Hope of truth and light, we do send out of soul, of hunger.

Give it to me

Mind disturbed of single shot ugliness, that lived place still
spinning, stressed of arts, thinking and pics, black matter tries
to defeat the will powered beauty of monster I have created,
but its to placid of strength to die down on knees, to give up to
you, so FUCK YOU!
Action of peace, love and kindness, on consistency, from my
troubled mind of personality, but I live on, to your gravity pull,
will not let myself knife off to the flying life of after, not on my
own accord, only by yours, my life of power and fate, I think?
Vibrations chime of talk, days flee by of emotions of pain and
love, let one know, you're still needed and wanted, by those
of life forms. Suns glimmer, moons shine, skies of colours lay
over, nature chirps and squeaks, I shall stay.
Give me the dark moments and suffers of those and mine, ill
handle with care, like ornaments of china, let the smiles
spread of light. You still suck of shite flies, but you have your
points of buttered nuggets, but we still live on with the
intention of, FUCK IT, THAT'S LIFE...!

Here's a bun

Feeling numb
A silent cum
Run Mandy run
This once assaulted gun
Now a broken one
He wants none
He wants none
Now here's a bun!

I

I pace this floor, time and time again
Wonder into fantasy
I watch a fly in a figure of eight
I taunt death to knock my door
I get no reply
I see a daddy long legs, take a seizure
I see a bug walk the pane
I am the superhero of all time
I am the beast that all hate
I am the I of all I

I know is real

Sunshine glare my face...
Fierce release!
Through this transparent glaze
Roll up... roll down!
These four walls consume my heart...
Watch why you crumble around me!
You have forsaken me...
Forgiveness I prevail!
The... dirt I know is real...

Karmatic roses

Sensitive skin
Touch me, I bleed
Hold me, I love
The fall of a strand, a little lock
Watch me cry and fall
Bent over from the pain
Hands holding my puzzle
I ask of the enemy… keep me straight
For your watchful eye has disgusted me
Throw my rubbish at your feet
With sunset dirt
Your choices of karmatic roses
Hands clasped so softly… I go
Scared to leave you on your own
Reunite and reincarnate
Your new life awaits
Smell the coffee and the roses!

## Little boy

I am not over you to say the least
My mind has gone weary and not at peace
The electric distortion has growing me apart
These strange thoughts and feelings, in my mind and my heart
Since you have gone I have got worst
But the flower inside me wants to ignite and burst
I have got lazy and fat
With the help of a pink twat
But I still want to flip my hat
My life is in chaos and destructive line
I don't know how much longer I can stay with you in this lifetime
For what I am doing to myself is selfish and very rude
Yet I am walking in a universal starry night and sunset tube
Living with amazement and of awe…
Yet the little doggy, still gives me a woof and her paw
Even though I would love to have you back
The burden I lay on you was enough and my back is weak from wearing this sack
I love you and miss you with all of my heart
I live with the memories of our bipolar love, from the end, until the start
My life will go on without you I know
Yet I will still cry out for you in the night, I know so…
Live happy and healthy my little petal of joy
For me… my life will be chained in the corner, sweat dripping my distorted soul and body of wounds, I will just stay a muffled and confused little boy
I know now after all this time
That the break up was for the best and it let us chime
Even though I had to let you go
It put me in an all-time low
But its time for you to spread your wings
And time for me to get on with things
Even though you have no idea I do this so
You are in my heart, my body… forever and I will never forget and let you go
This is me… the psychological puzzle
But my peace loving and kind heart holds this world of mine in a muzzle
Me… the little boy!

My heart of shame

Black hole submerge me so
The sweet serenity in my lobes
Drag, I drag in hope you see by…
My death of ashes happening
I don't know why I call your name
With my head held low
In my heart of shame
I'm sorry…

Prayer

Rub hands together
For I pray
Please take my hand one more time
So I can feel whole again
I lay in the bath
My tears fill me up
As I cry out your name!

Repent

Translucent body
Perfect sculpture
Diving deeper into the crusty core

Breathing oxygen severely
Living in fear, of being specific
Dying corrosively in acid of black

Help me Jesus, help me

The silence kills
Not even a whisper
I repent for my sin
For I am unhappy for the intent, I didn't intend

Forgive my stupidity!

Smile my friend smile

Walking lonely in the road
A smoke, a drag relieve me so
The thought of death and despair on my mind
The loneliness kills the nectar inside
Piss here, piss there
Under your forever stare
I want to sleep in the bed of forever
You say right now… never
My poetic song is running out of form
This life of mine, is not for the norm
Now I say my goodbyes, hopefully in a high
Have no more and bow out with a sigh!

Sparsely creative dot

My heart troubled
No direction
Lost in the sail
My touch, for you only
A puzzle with no solution
Creative sparsely
Eliminated through days and years
Need release
Yet no speak
Sedated in a trance
All that is wonderful has dissipated to a dot
No reality
No fantasy
Limbo is my name
Hail to all, for I am here
Bow with disgust and surprise!

## Star bright, star alight

Star bright, star alight, I look upon you, on the stainless
Star bright, star alight, tell me the truth
Star bright, star alight, you lied to me
Star bright, star alight, this wall is aching
Star bright, star alight, this fuzz is deranged
Star bright, star alight, when met, my name is serene
Star bright, star alight, there is no name
Star bright, star alight, there is no wall
Star bright, star alight, there is no fuzz
Star bright, star alight, only soul
Star bright, star alight, you have told me the truth
Star bright, star alight, you have not lied
Star bright, star alight, for I looked long enough this time
Star bright, star alight, I shall pass through the tip of the pin
Star bright, star alight, I shall play in your dream
Star bright, star alight, that's all we are, until the pitch!

## Strain

Feeling like a monstrous caged animal, on his own accord.
Knows he has the key of heart, to break free.
Scared to move up the hill of salvation.
Scared to stay in the unlocked house.
Fear of reversing back, like a car into a crash.
All because the black cloud of fear, sets in, over the creatures head.
Once a bird of freedom and life, now trapped, with his variety of destruction.

Mania sets in, feels like a dvd on fast forward, erratically skipping from scene to scene, going through too much information of thought to process, in his fine mind.
Feeling ready to pop like a red cherried balloon.
Depression sets in, like crawling through a claustrophobic tunnel, splintered in glass and heavily liquidised with bleach.

The creature performs his merely boring daily routine, of little existence.
Fakely grinning to those he knows, lying to himself and the ones he loves, sacrificing and comforting them like a night-time teddy bear.
So they do not know his suffering and get hurt, by his troubled mind.
He sits within his day to day, by a daze, feeling trapped within a mirror of the air he breaths, suffocating and dying.
The crisis moment lands and someone sets him free, a power he has not felt before but one stronger than thee.
They say, stop the disc and press play, you shall enjoy every moment, he say.
I give you the light at the end of your tunnel, so you can crawl a little further and you shall be free.
After all the strain he has experienced, he no more feels like a dirty, ugly troll.
He feels like the bird he once was before.
Balanced in the wind of his wings and taking life as it is!

## Stuck

Unhappy, depressed, walls closed in on your life, you feel
worthless, son talk. He set you free to your decision of life
changed forever, oh...
The insanity of attempt of forever clash, hospital and late
night punch of flowers and bees that enfolded. We didn't
expect, but hugged with hearts of gold, we emotionally
sorrowed with a headache of torture and a light touch of
actions.
Heartbroken, torn and shattered, loneliness and confusion,
oh... the unit has broken, WHAT TO DO?
Sick she was, from the dark demons of dusty cloud for weeks,
like a cancer, TEAR =[ the constant chitter chatter of ear,
ready to fall, we listen and we hold arm's length in middle. So
there's no earthquake of red, with a twister of awkwardness.
Oh please stop, OH PLEASE, were stuck, STUCK!
Even though all has parted each way of chosen line of curves,
twists and smiles, the tension still bears on the rusted, broken
crown, that's on museum of years to see and come of talk, for
life-time of us all!
One my best friend of angel and the other my friend, I be
there for both. No judgement, no hard feeling, for all that is
done is done, that was to be, for us all. WE MOVE ON!

Sugar life

To touch is to destroy
To say is to hurt
To move is momentum towards destruction
My own
My self
The I
Of all there is to be of me
I call out
Never to be heard
By that they call the one
Please hear my cry
Of desperation
Carry my load
Towards a sugar life
That there be for me
HEAR MY ROAR...!

Little Boy

Summer grief

With summer grief
Rain drip my smile
Where are you sunshine
My lips tasted with this grip and denial

Cut inside a cardboard box
The razor sharpened and slides against my wrist
Oh god, why have you forsaken me, as I clench
Let my life twist

I am but a disturbed and tortured little boy
But god, please hold my hand
Let this petal of life, be of joy

For these battles you commence me with, are dirty and very
cheap
But I lay by my bedside and pray
And hope you hear me as I weep

For my faith in you, used to be so high
Now so low
I look at you as a lie

You get those to do as you please
The honest question is...
Do you even exist?

I will rip this body and mind to shreds
Let my soul simmer and greet those with ease

For the darkness will turn no evil in me
My heart of soul is golden
It is rich in molten alchemist
Let all see the angel in me

I hope one day I will hold this down, like the leopard to the
deer
Cry out for help
Look out for those lightning signs
As I lay in the bathtub smoking, with a shiny tear

I will no more be a failure
Rip this life to pieces, with apathy and pens
I will sail these waters with the universal skies
As the unusual sailor

Yet this fire of burning, ceases to exist
Yet my lovers, it will come with excitement and vengeance
As hot coils on the fire
For now I will live this life diluted and in a mist!

Summer romantic strawberries

I cry
I shout
I laugh
I scream

Can IT really hear me?
Me is a question in itself
Do I really exist or am I just pretend?
Sane of the thoughts and feelings in my floating head

The pain, the sorrow hurts so bad
The happiness sends my heart into electrical glad

Peaceful moments in my life
I cherish like new plucked strawberries, in a romantic night

I will be happy moving on
Being distilled with happy ending Disney!

## The disturbed boy

His lean muscular body, sculpted like angelos david, fitness of
a lion, enduring after its prey, strength of a community of ants,
building their home of branches.
A soul of an angel, specifically chosen, from the heart of god's
faith!
A mind of dark and light, the raptures of evil, collide with the
greatness of good.
Those rough texture sweets, brings forth to him, the
tranquillity of living, day to day, instead of the heart throbbing
shakiness, the bat life and the game of pinball moods.
The faith of a few beautiful friends, close and afar. Lean upon
him, the responsibilities of angel work, of this planet of reality
dimension, like he is meant to cradle this baby, that is HIM!
He does not want that infant mind of trouble, he does not
know what to say or do.
That charm and charisma that was once him, of simplicity, is
no longer, it is disturbia and complexity, of life alive.
He knows he's on call of fate; he would have ended up mad
or suicidal dead long ago, if it wasn't for hi optimistic hope.
So he wavelengths on, with his soul of mid-melting iron, body
of chameleon and mind of affection.
He is, the disturbed boy!

## Tree

Tree with weary roots
Sustenance of drip and glow
Kissing those juicy lips
Syrup to my cone of cream
A thick trunk
Wind of breaking branches
Sap from the skin
Leaves shall die and fall

## Umbrella

Put up your umbrella
Its raining

Graze my tender face
You melt my heart
Yet your embrace is long gone
I just can't let you go

Put up your umbrella
Its raining

A downfall
My cheeks soak
Yet I live in parallel universes
My valves weakened, I died

Put up your umbrella
Its raining

In my silence, you are still heard and felt
It is golden
Look at me
Kiss me softly, one last time

Put up your umbrella
Its raining

Not even a whisper, from your shallow voice
It kills the nectar inside
Why for is this?
Yet I know you're scared to cross this line

Put up your umbrella
Its raining

There is faith in chaos
A message from a known stranger
The wait of anticipation
For like maybe to love

Put up your umbrella
Its raining

We are ghetto boys

Tranquillity so far away
I lurk in the back alleys, were I like to play
The black shadows surround my day and night
Though my gin and juice, in hand, is only at sight
My steel attire keeps me safe as I walk in the crowd, without a
wave
I am only angry and frustrated as my fist is clenched and walk
this pave!

## Where you at?

Once upon a second gone by, let the fairytale end and the
consciousness awaken!
The smoke of reality is assumed, to those clean lungs of
carefree function and the black holes of questioning, clinch
on, like demons on angel self, trying to do good1
The cups of tea, wish I didn't take all that sugar, because I'm
watching my figure and on the box of representing.
Using the sphere, under the brown infinite blanket, as a
chicken feed, of high rate, mass produce products, in a hurry.
To keep it all under control and in their power!
Where's the freedom, the justice, the individuality?
Even the rebellion has become a form of ediqit. There's no
expression no more, there's just no expression no more,
where you at?

Without a whisper

Two nights, of fuzzy ecstasy
With all in front of me
Yet you will slip faintly into the night
Without a whisper

Open wounds

So petty for letting these open wounds torture me for all this
time of years, like shite to my fur.
For I am a freedom spirit of defence
This time of hour has changed my perception of these open
wounds
I know they will open and shut through all of me
Though my infinite chance has, is and always will be there, to
close for explore and rest to play
But I live here!

## Momentarily relapse

The black smoke surrounds and floats in my sub...
Will it? Or will I?
I'm talking to a brown red bird on a shovel, by a waterfall
Please answer my question of my broken red base?
Always a rucksack to a starry blueish dark night...
Can you let me know that this is where I am going?
Though I see this hundreds and thousands of a feathered
silhouetted angel, gracefully gliding and guiding, as you stand
from flight, eight foot tall over my shoulders!
Even though I know and do this life, there is always a knick of
this...
Momentarily debilitating of inspired relapse!

The story of the bowl

You comfort me last night
Sugary sip crunch
You lay in the shitter
Now just a sour slurp to my lumps
That's the story of the bowl!

Painful purpose

A haunted argument
Followed by a detailed explanation of a shag you haven't
even had or imagined
A message from a guru, to release you of this excited
depression
To put purpose to this pain!

You're a powerful presence that you can't even see or feel
A leader of millions of this one self
That will guide dew north, through the seasons
In a difficult cleanse

A breezeful piss and a finger up to your closeness, to leave
you alone to stew with the barrel in the mouth!
Fuck off... fuck you off and fuck me off
PLEASE...!
This energy crumbles me to the point of creative destroys!

Hairy trousers

A process to the darkest pitch of near death!
At Saturday night... dickhead at live
Now sober I have become alive, awake and aware of the
philosophies in tune!
Don't take offence... it's a spiritual thing... you wouldn't
understand through shallow!
I'm not judging you because... I am the man with the hairy
trousers
You're in a process you can't stop but remember if it takes
grip... you're addicted!
For what you see is all you and its only self-judgement you
must proclaim!
For I am a man with two faces here right now...
A contradict and a dedicated!
Take my word once and by then... I've messed up this!
Intentionally I'm fighting through the four journeys, up and
down, with tenacious learning sequence!
Forgive me if I stumble, in my hairy trousers!

Little Boy

Inspirational nightmare!

Your life is an inspirational nightmare and it goes like this....

Half hazed from tinted sun
Sipping on a hot milky beverage and a smokey pear...!

Disgust aroma shoes in a hat rack sweat

Heavier kilogram stones than before, getting cock sucking
from red flowered, sticky shorts!

Brown swimming swamp to a star in this heaven
We reach too which is you
With the depressed aura without spoke...
From a melted screen towards alcohol, jealous suicide!

A windful hair, with a nervous system, straight service to the
brain...
Now...
This is not just a black and a white carved scripture, as awake
This is...
And now I'm trying to be ignorant!

Intentional determination

Narcissistic to the blunt point
You have taking a skate to OZ, to meet the king!
Hello…
Hello…
Blunt to the point my lady
Your narcissistic guzzle on this page…
A scripture you have not created because of a child ill
expression, from squeezed social peers!
Now you face Lucifer shakily and infectively bust!
Goodbye my lady…
Because you have blankly slated and wiped to mold
another…
Through intentional determination
But you will always be my wee ice-cream, cradled in
bubblewrap, from ill peer intentional determination!

She's a dreamer

3 AM and your hanging round my neck, like I was after upset
at 5am before!
Just a bounceful karma
There like a fence, only now we have to break, for my
girlfriend's tears torn apart and crumble on the grass!
A burning passionate heart, in her wombful growth
She's in a deadly comfort, with sparotic responsibilities
Great in the eyes of others but not great in her own…
reflected reflection!
She's a dreamer… only in the wrong way, with a suicidal push
goodbye!

"misguided angels"

Beautiful motion

Ice cream birdcage
Crackled and shattled
Microscopic energy
Puff and blew
Tsunami of beautiful motion
Rumbled starvation
Gained spirit
As I wrap my arms warmly around you
Ice creamed cage opens
Bird of determination
Fly with heart...
Climb the ladder and gain a star for you, in the night
The white knight!

Chicken beaks and horse hooves

Inhale your cancerous cells to my breathing box
Loneliness outshines me in these parts
Dark penetration eludes self
I am in silence
My door does not knock
My sleep uninterrupted
My feelings strong and muffled, as I wake
One day I will find that voice
I will not condemn myself of that beautiful existence!

## Circle Of Angels

As I sit here,
As still as a mirror,
Taken in every little detail,
Amongst these circle of angels,
That dance in the heavens above,
I feel warmth,
That is love and creative energy,
That burns like a wild fire in my heart.

In a circle there is but everlasting life,
And in this case a friendship,
With closeness,
That's compacted like a bunch of wild flowers.

In our circle of friendship,
There is no such thing as a higher diplomat or lower economy
We are but one equal,
Drawing on a fine line of 180 degrees.

Thank you my circle of angels,
For this everlasting creative energy,
Love and equalness,
That we draw onto one another,
Like a bee to the pollen of a flower,
Thank you my CIRCLE OF ANGELS.

Come out of your shell

Temporary shell
Forever light
Torn or destroy
Growth or life
A decision of whisper choice
There is no matter in the corruption
For it is pure; when sloth
For the spots are what we do
A cake of mush
Or
Brighter glow
Though in this line; only intention is love
It is divine!

## Complete Elizabeth bliss

Lay here beside you in complete Elizabeth bliss
Your breaths as you sleep, is my life with love
My devotion to you is pure
I do my best by you
Being me is enough for you
You say with delight in your voice

Discreet

Blue sky
Open moon
Coffee and coke
Fat drips and suckles
These shadows choke

Flooded ocean fields
Laughter in smile
Wind chimes bang
A breezeful walk
Every moment sang

Noisy pink laces
A purple cushion pouch
A balloon pen pierced hole
Miniscule of light
Walk this path of sole

Dwarfed in blackness
Star shining line
Voice so soothing
In discreet with wizard wands
Higher condensity moving...

Dog poop

Swallow cack
Gung the teeth and run
A misunderstood genius
She twirls the cushion dough, with red puke
The green lights and all smiles
Embrace the impossible
Ordinary have done
Adventurous dogs
Smooth sailings
Now is where I turn to
Because of you!

Dream

Climb the apple snowflaked roof
Slide down the cinnamon spaghetti ledge and eat
Wash it all down
With spring onion flavoured water!

Enjoy

Fallen from the heavens
Crash and bang off the rooftops
The wind through my hair and face
Enjoy the downfall
As it trickles my cheeks
Enjoy!

Flame ignite

Slow damp of death, in this heart of mine
Slowly dying of no ignite
There is more in these bones, than lets on to be
This is all art
Ready to learn at every corner
Though we all will be in the sleep of bed forever
Let the spark ignite and lead me to my fate
I will find you and marinate to a delicious produce
With a smiley face!

Letting me go!

Egg of safety, closed from it all, hatch I come, let the real come in with a breeze of release, watch me grow as you feed and comfort me, let me go and find my sustenance, as I build up, as you watch on.

One fine let me go, to take this confusion of philosophy on, as I get hurt with pain and sorrow, with goodness and sun smiles.

I hope we meet again, for the hot steaming cuppa, in your new nest, miles away from mine.

But you are still half my heart; love you for letting me go!

Little solider

I see you little solider
I feel your every move
I want and have been you little solider
I see your beautiful face
I know I want you!

## Lollipop dynamite

Hold freely or ignite the dynamite
A lollipop or an explosion
The bunny crawls and wails
Infected finger touches out
Condemned with dishonesty and hurt
The bunny licks and laughs
The sweetened perfumed finger touches out
Inspired only with goodness and love!

Lonely room

A tainted opaque aura
A lonely room
Two lonely cups
Two lonely chairs
Empty after the chitter chatter
A single sensitive rub
One star ready to explode
Glistening bells
A stammered and hesitated kiss…to start
A smoke by… now joint
From a razors cut, to a feathers touch!

## Mite

Mite..mite..mite-bite
Fly to the temple
Illuminated black coffee
Red rim of death
Run it out
Till the thread is thin
So the rubbish can sinfully slam into the bin

Put a lid on it
Fire it up
Burn it all night
Get it out of my sight
Soon I will put it all right!

Ours and all mine

I take you in my hand
Hold you with care
Fill myself with the warm fuzziness to my heart
That we once shared.

Will never let you go
You will always hold a special place in the shadow of my alive
With immense glow.

I will move on
All in goodtime
We will share with a smile and a frown
Something that we can call...
Ours and all mine!

## Pin

A pin in the finger
As the joker makes his talk
A peeing audience laughs
He is weak at their disapproval
A met eye with fear in the heart
A somersault of affection, in a narcissistic display
Take my hand, I am peter and together we will fly
In New York we shall jump with sweets, in delight
He does not know his line
The show must go on
Laughter he gets with the blurp, behind the mask
Pinks for calms as he looks at the numbers
Pull out the pin

Thickly still

Fired up
Fired up
A steaming cup, sets me off
Sugar to my noose
Hang me up
Lower me down
Thickly still
Bear the juicy lips
Come out like smell!

## This

This crippling death
This magnetism of spark
This road of light and dark
This is a joke in the evil eyes of this smudgy dimension
This is a seriousness of serenity
In the eyes that gleams
I am a troll under this bridge
Hiding from the light, of this day
I am the troll of the night that brings me out of my shell
No one can see me for my ugly self is too taunting
Underneath this layer of fur and dirt
I am more…
A chain ties me but I am more than your eye beholds
Wipe away all that you see
Look into my daring eyes of greenness
Look at my smile
See how my fur can gain you warmth and peace?
Take this chain from me and let me free
I will show you how much of a lovely person, I can be!

## Violet

You are the queen that was introduced to my heart early, a fresh fragrant to my humanly senses, a colour so radiant, it can be seen from this universal life, of never ending.

Unfortunately your throne was upon me, in my darkness, so I did not act, but that behind us now, it looks like the connection of likeness, has stood the test of time!

When I seize hold a connection, with my eyes, at your light pink, robust, flamboyancy, I can see that those features, release me of my darkest hours and shine through, like the sun, in an august afternoon.

You are the rose of my heart, my life, my violet!

Waken up

Wake to a cup of black
Blowing rings
Kings of music

Hold the love close over voice-transmitter and written cyborg
Or
Hold to touch with my sensitive toasted heart
And
Ride the still or splashy concrete
With wheels or fins!

My forever bloom

Blue ocean, tainted blood
Seep my bones
Just a dirty troll
Darkness fills this room, of shut blind
I'm I just a fool?
Soon to be forgotten and lost with your slippery grasp
Please... oh please. Love me like no other in this time
I prefer me sedated in your embrace
This is a fucking joke ha ha
But love is all around and a forever circle of being
Though in this evil
Eyes down
Chin to chest
I stare into oblivion
Let the music end with words
For one day, my persona will end as a hero
For what is inside, will burst
My forever bloom!

The peaceful descendent

The train stammers on its line
It reaches my decision
Smashes into me like rain and crushes me in wet paint
Pleasant devotion
Though corruption is marbles in my veins
Sedated and in your arms
Close to your heart
The creative spirit still lives on
This unique universe pickles my box
Though I live with a smile and frown, in its comfort and pain
I learn from the fairies, as they touch me with their magic
wands
I hear only a hero can defeat these demons now
Will I be the superior?
Will I die in this echoed shattered silence?
With love and recognition
There will be a peaceful descendent...

snowballs

Snowballs avalanching down the mountain top, like chocolate flaked ice cream topped cones, with hundreds and millions slaughtered on my fairy cakes, why… oh so why, is this life fucked up, and why… oh so why is it so fucked up for me, please give me the answers you one holy son of a god damn gun!

Hehe not really, oh.. Please not really, if I had those jellybean toppings on my hot chocolate, I am for sure to go insane in my marshmallow! Oh.. But how we asks these enigmas, but really we do not the answers, but there is a part of you that would love thee explanations, but seriously, would you like to be stared at, in the streets of civilisation, as an outcast and a fucking weirdo, hmmmmmmmm?

She uses her tickle tips, gliding them down his neck, as she watches him giggle out load, as she rubs her walker on his stiff structure, getting his blood to the tip, ready to blow.… He rubs his labours over her moisturised skin, all over, with sensation of his beat boxer, he moves down the ladder, covered at her, with denim and leathered studs, he slips it off, to caress her hollowed thumping cave, bats aloud, she yelps with pleasure of confidence and suspense, a scream of satisfaction, I LOVE YOU BABY!!!! =]

Ecstasy disappearing from it all, fantasy he yawns in from stars of reality, but to be boot in face from the hand of it all, his face droops from smile, and pleasure becometh the pain in mind and body, he travels on with stiff neck and clenched hands, till next time the dream plane takes him away to the next kick of trip in life a journeyed a lived in mist and factuation…

Little Boy


Because of you

You flow into me, like a river overflowed with the beating
beads of rain and the wind whizzing by….

I LIKE YOU, I LOVE YOU…

You help create my creativity, with your screaming room of
vibrations, with only me there,
Interrupted sleep
My dark moods
Blinds shut
And the pulsating disturbed heartbeats of anxiousness!

The light of ying, inspiration to motivate of temporary action,
creates the art pieces of expression, of a life lived in a
storytelling environment of love, hate and serene!

I DON'T LIKE YOU, I FUCKING HATE YOU…

Your journey of stars, never gives me a chance to rest; it
makes my life a living hell.

But…

I wouldn't have it any other way, only so few of us can take
you for so long of period, people have suicidally died
Because of you
Others have hurt
Because of you!

But… my strength of will, shall not be tempered with, I control
you, I accept you.

You're my friend, my enemy and my acquaintance on the
street of socialization.

Chaos – yang!

## Coming back to you lily

Wired birds and minted flossed bees, here I come, on the road
again, with a frown of fear and excitement of glee!

Puppy cloud be aware, my blue smoke is in the air, as we speak of
non-sense and think of the one I miss, love with purest and damaged
heart, we sit with thought!

Click-clock across the layered stone, come with me petal of my
heart, take my hand, into this arch of grace I feel, step through with
me, feel... what is that?

It's the snowdrop flowers, that sit at the welcoming, the watching of
others habits and behaviours, it is the ray of light, that beats off my
back, it is the expression, this ink and paper, help me feel and the
coffee I sip with caution labelled, but...

Foretell... all this and everyone here, its nothing like you and nor is it
you soulfully, the happiness you make me feel, the questioning, I
question, of self? That you help me see, I'm full of more bloom, than
I can imagine, but on forth, in told, you help me feel all of emotions in
ecstasy, of all accord and all I can hope for, is that, I help you this
way also...

Dream I do... laying with me, cuddled in my arms, kiss my neck, feel
my body, touch my mind and connect with my soul, I only want you,
forever my heart says, you are my medicine for life, I need you...!

Lost in the middle of this smudge, a lonely but cupped little boy and
man, tick-tock the clock goes, I'm having fun as I said I would and
now the doors are opened, its time for me to grow, hopefully... with
you!

The early sunshine chimes, awakens me glistenly from my sleep, my
paper by my side, to rescue my hearts peace, I kiss my substitute for
you!

The fuel goes down the hatch, with steady velocity, before I make
my way through the serenity and anxiousness of hill-tops, mountains
and dark tunnels, but I anticipate to see you again, the smile on my
face and the butterflies say it all, I'm coming back to you lily and I
just can't wait!

## My Wild Girl

As I passively walk my daily retreat,
I gaze from my peripheral vision,
Upon a queen so alluring,
It makes my heart tremble of clarity.

There is a woman in front of me,
Skin so smooth,
I could polish my finest jewellery on.

Her hair silk, brown, short and sleek,
Hanging on her shoulders weightless,
It radiates, with a hat to cover,
Just enough, so one doesn't get blinded,
Of its elegance.

Those clothes she wears,
On that delicate and fimble body of hers,
Calls out to me,
"EXPRESSION OF SELF".

As she is tunnel visioned to that wild purple flower,
Seeking its meaning of existence,
Only if she knew that flower is a mirror reflection,
Of her beauty in my eyes.

The flowers potency shines,
Just like her,
Without one of those flowers on that bush of magic and
mystery,
The structure of it would fall apart forever,
As would my life and the entire world,
If this gorgeous creature was vanished off it.

As she cracks her smile,
It's like the flowers open wider,
Their bee attracting middle is an eye,
In order to grasp hold of,
With their flowery minds,
One of life's many wonders,
"HER".

Unfortunately I know that this moment will only be short lived,
As like many great moments in our lives,
But I have lived the moment and she,
"MY WILD GIRL",
shall stay with me on my days of dreams and reminiscence,
"MY WILD GIRL".

# Little Boy

My predator in the woods

As you and me were friends in our so called teenage lives,
Our greatest years our peers tell us so,
Like an old wives tale,
We struck around on our skateboards,
Kick flipping our way through together,
From dusk till dawn.

We went through a lot together,
Sweet scented girls,
The bitter taste of alcohol,
The fanticistic drug taken,
And scheming those death defying days of school,
But one faithful day you flipped like a coin,
In our 4th year of paradise,
Soon to be hell.

One day,
One week,
A month,
A year,
2 years had passed by like a bird in the wind,
And you developed a cyst of a grudge,
Ugliness and,
Anger against my expressive soul,
It was unforgettable,
Those days of torture,
But you helped me create something I wasn't,
"A REVENGER".

I ravishly trained every day from the early morn,
To the midnight moonlight,
To develop myself into a dirty troll of revenge and aggression,
In order to confront you my sworn enemy,
"YOU FUCKER".

I got off those heavy, steel, cold weights,
And that blood stained bag every day,
With hands tortured with blisters and,
Callus the size of oranges,

My legs screamed in agony when I ran,
This pain was placed with you in mind,
You 6ft tall monstrous, sleek of piss,
"WHAT IM I DOING?"


To my surprise one day I realized,
That I have let myself waste 3 years of my life on you,
And forgot about my life, "YOU",
I want it back, but I can't,
I read and read about life,
To find out my solace,
I've got it…
"FORGIVENESS"…


But this is so hard,
And so difficult,
As it churns in my stomach like a blade stuck in a washing
machine,
As I think about it,
It makes running barbed wire threw my skin,
Feel like cake on a Sunday afternoon.


What pretentious fuckers believe I can do this?
To a man who tortured and helped cause me pain for years,
Inside and out,
Who are these fuckers?
Taoists, Buddhists, Christians, Ghandi,
It's all just holy crap,
That's what I say,
Fuck them,
Why not a good right on the jaw?
"HEY"?


They tell me that it gives me power within,
More like they should bend down and suck my cock,
These one-dimensional dolly birds,
But I am a man of experimentation,
I must try,
I seek for enlightenment.…


What's this, what's this?
Feelings of joy and happiness I receive as I forgive and let go,

## Little Boy

I've realized this is the power they tell me,
People and all these things around me,
I see bundles of love and energy,
I want more....

I forgive you, I love you, I forgive you, I love you,
My journey has started,
I must venture more into this love and vibrance,
I am a good person full of,
Peace, love and kindness,
Opened for my new life lessons in these categories of light,
"MY FRIEND I FORGIVE YOU".

Baby

The nectar inside me has died
But…
I promise I will never let your heart sink into the ice as mines
has
Your soul will melt the sun!
In this silence our love is still felt
Through this dark that you have so gracefully helped me
through…
Your love has been felt.
Your hand so tightly gripped to mine and you have never let
me slip so far into hell…
You have introduced me to heavenly happiness
Now through our optimistic plans together
The light will shine and the flowers will open in the spring, with
our hearts
Together…forever!

Enter to snuggles and kisses baby!

The devil has taken a death grip
Though I am in your trance
My love for you is Disney ending
I will have many flickered rose petal romantic nights for you
For your love is worth it baby
Some people say romance is dead but not from my heart or
mouth
You're my lady of luck and light
A forever held hand is this cycle
Meet me in heaven and we will dance for eternity
For I am happy in this darkness
Because of your amazement!

For now... I have you!

Two doves fly holding hands
God has created with perfect heart
Cuddled into me
The love as pure as snow
As it falls from the heavens
A tearful delight trickles my cheek
I smile like the clowns
The hug
The kiss
Brings out the glow in my soul
Forever I intend to hold your hand
For now... I have you!

## Holiday

Opaque is the window to my heart as you are gone from the
comfort orbit
Hands still clenched to yours as you left my door
Wave goodbye with a smile though the frown is expected as
you go!
Crushed is the dust under my skin, as it is swept away
Thinking of you as I pray to my god
To look after you every step of the way
The feeling so potent on you
As I dream of you all night away!
I know I will be with you one day soon and the window of my
heart will be transparent again!

I have always known

As I walk gracefully in the grass
You sit out to me like a purple tulip teardrop
Breathe in the fresh air with me and enter solace together
Holding heart to heart
Shut our eyes in this silence and we are in heaven
We shall eat chocolate and drink coke in this timeless form
Our love radiates to the misguided and lost
They see what true love is and baby…
That is us!
The thing is…I have always known…that you are the love of
my life!

My baby

A glowing tube of light through the heart
Rich endorphins seduce my body
My tampered mind never so clear
My baby... my life... my holism
The darkness buried
The now, so in light and love
The future so planned in precision.... With flow!
I will make my baby so in grin
So in love
Be my goddess of energy, circling my world and my universe!

## Spring

With this spring in my step
My heartbox filled with butterflies
Each time I look into your eyes the love fills me up
Through my pain there is always a get well wish from your
heart!
You know any pain of yours shall always be relieved by me
I will not let a tear trickle your cheek
You shall always smile in my arms
This is our spring
We shall always have depth
We shall always have fun
We shall always have spring in our hearts as we let each
other know…
We love us!

The light of the doves

Spring has arose in my heart
These stable clouds have parted
To let the sunshine dart upon us
For you have held my hand tightly through this nightmare of
terrors
I will hug you closely
I will kiss your ruby lips
I promise never to let your hand carelessly slip from mine
I need you always in this life
For the dove in this light will guide us to grow old together
Holding hands
Forever and ever!

We are ok!

Anatomy muscly teeth swallowed me up and I am dead
But...
Awoken in a nerve panic
Breathing sharply
You were there to rest me!
Grabbing the snowed goatee
But...
I pulled your hair
Now you are mad
But...
We can't for too long
For it bleeps
For it boils
For the door slams
But... I still smell your hidden fragrance on my cardigan
We are ok!

# Little Boy

"sex, anger and depression!"

Beg

Rape of innocence
Swift of pain
Hand covered in shit
Blood drip my tears
The shadow lurks my path
In the centre of it all
Dreamcatcher out to you… and see what you swallow up?
Stand fright still!
A blackout and severed will only gather
Its no solution
Sweat it out in the ball
Gather these shoes for selection
Swallow the blood liquid sludge
Turn to it on knees and beg for it, with metalled hands
Golden liquor my crevices…
Broken and damaged…
Now I am an everlasting diseased love

Careless love

Crystal glaze as you walk in front of me
An angel I have seen
My first love...!
Drowned by many bacteria and a careless... I love you!
Just to say it with no meaning or bum
Just to make you comfortable and at ease
My head was not right but my intentions of heart were good!
I don't want you to be just another
I want you to be the one
I'm fed up for searching for these orgasms
Its time I settled down and got it on track!

## Confessions

A sinful chemical imbalance
Soul ever so grieving for opportunity?
Holistically weighted and clogged now!
Numb to the ignorance, after all this time!
These confessions shall waken us up!
Cheated by those I have trusted and by god?
I blame this everyday with sworn religion!
It has all started before I even knew, I was blissful, but... not anymore!
This is my confessions with no barrier reef...!

A sparkled swollen member in mouth
Tampered by one to the others
That makes this so hard to work with you, because of the deranged!

A headlock in the playground, to show you who is boss
A ghost has appeared in my streets and I carry this everywhere I go
It's not that I haven't tried in this soft venture
I should have smashed your faces into the concrete!

My friend of drunken and popping intention, has this miscarriage led you to believe in nothing?

Who am I to judge?
This attempt, as of yet, I have not attempt... only felt!
With steaming, blackout blue glow, in this sphere!
For myself... this suicide awaits from this ridiculous pain...!

Damage my vinyl, ill damage your god!

A timeless lawed rush
See in and see out
But you will go stagnant
If you don't gush

This foundation you so loudly speak
When layed at tender age and hoping it will bring all
Though I'm cast out and called a freak

For these creative problems I have rod
Please don't speak down to me of them
For I may not be at this peak right now
But I tell you this…
Damage my vinyl.. ill damage your god!

Dusty- trail

A dusty-trail left bare
A corner eyed glance
What is love?
You do not see what I see!
You do not feel what I feel!
A smile for a moment but for now...
This moment...
I will shed a tear for your darkness path!
Forgiveness for my guilt
Jerked out and squirt
The sculpture was set years ago
This quick placement on both of us was not planned; it was slammed by the chin!
I love you always and forever but this is never-ending and I'm sorry!
Don't live with it but I don't want you to discard it!
Walk this dusty-trail and see what prevails with us!
A fag later and us has died momentarily in this relapse...
Will we pick ourselves up from doggy-style?
We are now and back to front...
Only then do we orgasmically live though we love in all ways!
Alarming clocked up with it all
Just love me like no other...as I will!
Dream as I dream
Cast to the ocean of the unknown
Build the rheumatoid sculpture soothing
Talking through the couch forever more
Disintegrate this through this dusty-trail laid bare!

Fairy-tale

Once upon a time…
This isn't no fairy-tale
A damsel in distress
Wipe a tear with a borrowed napkin
That used to be self-owned with love and affection
This horror two masked man crying for fake orgasms
You do not know this hidden man but shoot on shot!
A can too many
Skin as yellowman
As in holidays
The smoke is all life and bone
Never to surface from this tainted sacrifice
Live happily ever after
The end…!

Grit your teeth

A vast love of tubed toothpaste
Coming into me at small quarters
It's never taken its time before but this time with whole
heart...
I have to make sure!
Did it begin?
Will it end?
Tip-toe beat with smile
Crash or tumble of frown
The sipping tea has come out to me
From that foundation...
I know how to take it now!
Don't hide your emotions away
Be like the dove and fly to the bay.

Ice cream blowjob

Butterflies and spiders
Candy canes and snow
Burst the balloon with a banana

In the rusty trail

Blackout… white paws in the rusty trail
A chocolate cream skin
You have fallen on me so seasonal
Latch a crutch for the last time
My advice is simple but simple
True though…
As of love and loss
Where is honest self?
Now a sparkle smoke as I watch without talk…
Though in this frequency, you work within the common social
behaviour
STOP…!
Wide open, taking it all
No cum to spit
Still so young and not producing
Vengeance of suicidal puff, will be mines
Scared to walk this familiar space
Butterflies of anxious anger
KILL YOU, YOU HATEFUL BASTARD!
You're not the only one
I do not believe a single word or story you mention anymore!
None of you
Fuck you all!
A hermit crab in my own home
I cry these numbness tears
Need these seductive sedatives right now?
SAMS is my name in the rusty trail
Now we are over
Shake my hand proudly and that conditioned hug
We are over in the rusty trail!

It's a stepping stone dream

A thanks too many for this terrible man!
You have ran away from my heart
I have never loved you as much as I do right now!
For my life is tidal tide shore, irregular and unnormal
You handle with porcelain care and I shall never forget you for
that!
We nearly parted our ways
Just the other days!
Shall prophecy be true... you will never be cornered alone!
My exhausted hung out to dry... will always look after you!
Gazing old... though forever seeking new
Caffeine smoke is killing me, of your very worst fear
I'm SORRY...!
Low to the fact that I cannot prevent
When upstairs is ready?
Kill my bright... for it will be right!
A for distance memory concluded now...!
Star shines with glow, now and on!
Potent from source and excuses no more...
Time is all and is...
It's all just a stepping stone dream!

## It

As we lay in this steam
Goosebumps on my skin
Crumbled under the fear
Covered in my sheets

There are only so many places to hide
Tonight my friend
Here comes the tide

Not a vengeful fist
Hot coals will perch you tonight
Universally it's been on the list

We shall see you in heaven
I shall hug you to your next carnation
Kiss your honey lips
Till they fall off!

Killing me with kindness

Ride the rocking chair
Shave the blade
A light bulb drips
Fuck you
Fuck you
You vindictive bastards
My head on a wire
I hate this
Molten leaded gold I do
I love you is all I say
Arms out...
Huggles and smooch
You're killing me with your kindness!

Nirvana heal me!

I will say hello when you come my way but I shall hate your
stay
Thankful when we say goodbye
Brushed up against your green nettle with thick hairy skin
Dissolve into me and I shall become white
Is it worth it?
For unknown…what I will see on the other side
I feel threatened by your company
For you have kissed her once but don't worry or pickle
For I want to die
I am already dead
For these electric signals have…
Hurt and pain is all I have been seduced too!
So nirvana…heal me?

## One time

A fear so potent
A punch to the throat
Knocked out right now from just one
Never too be conquered
For this is too violent
For reputation of personality consistent!
Will care with persistence
Die alone from where its innocence raped and warned illusion
started!
Your breath in my can
Touched by invisible
This brand new, now start!
Tremble later but not this usual!
A test from every time and in everyday!
Bringing me down anymore… its time to escalate for me…
With love and justice!

## Opaque

I got into a relationship so fast
How come I keep lurking into the past?
I don't remember the last time I felt sane
But oh boy I remember this pain
A pin and a prick it hurts
Buddha calls out to me and burps
A deep slumber is what you say so
My friend there must be more? I know so
For I have smelt the grass in the wind and have felt the
smothering heavenly touches
Your theory and concerns have muches…
It has to be opaque?

Perfumed hourly space

Hand open wide
Tripping on diluted juice
Zigzag interpreted despair
Climbing slippery down the soaking slope
I cry my heart out as I am wailing to the distance shining
Nothing takes me to the heavens gates
Rusted cut off and there will be no more of this but I need it to
survive in this!
Angry buzzy bees swim in the tampered oceans
They do not last long in this perfumed hourly space
Disintegrate the red and I and all...will have peace!

## Pinebox

Tired, sick, headache…
Caused all by my heartache
Sit with me in silence
A squeeze with no sound
Listen…?
I am afraid
Help me?
I can't go on
Hang me from the bridge
Blow a hole in my heart
My soul has died
No love
This confusion has departed me from this reality
I live in fantasy
Searching for balance
How's this going to work?
Do you even understand?
Of course not!
Nobody does!
It's invisible
I caused yours and mine!

Playing the victim

Playing victim
My sister in heaven
Ignite from this
Life so hard
Never meant for you!
Weep from the emotional stone inside
I know you hear me weep from grandpas shaking knee?
Forgive my blessed stupidity
For not living in expectations all this time?
Now severe alone and confused
Time to pray for you!
This non-carnivore universe, was not your destiny
Better place now..!
I HOPE?
My rented goodbye will only be short
For I must live twice for you and me!
Natural happening
When and how is our mystery? But I am sure
For we are all!

Soft too the blow

Soft too the blow
A hard hitter
A monster of throw-down cuddling
Yet so soft too the blow

the aura of love will be there for you
it will crush you
hard on them, crushed to everyone but do not forget the little
ones!
The pain will not last but it will be momentarily lasting.

I don't want help?
A unique star...
The blizzard perish...
For this lasting disease
Times have cherished early in comfort with me... myself and
all!

Talk will only be when spoken questions
The answers are only stabilized lied... for my closet

Love in anger
Lost belief in segment
Will there ever be faith?
Your gunned lie has ended here!

For how long?
Presence in the ink
Truth and honesty!
Though in imbalanced anger
Cradle this new born
A strainful existence
It all goes too dust

So be soft too the blow!

## Solitaire

Below and down under
Darkness creeps
Lay in the dreambox
He is dying corrosively
Hit him please
Shake this shite clean out of him
He turns to ashes
Swept away by the wind of the night
Peacefully clean and in solitaire light!

The cast and spell

Forever life through mantra
Then why can't we make forever life?
The cast and spell of this we cannot escape
Take precautions but why?
For were born, live and die anyways!
No matter how big or small I am... I will decease!
Though you want us to live through love but you are one
bastard and cunt that destroys and stops!
Where's the faith?
Though to hurt is to self-harm
I totally understand that loneliness is my creative spark but
can't control when I'm gone in there!
I will never be happy with this
Forever more the dull seduces
Don't bark... for I will not order!
Sedate me from this shame and guilt
I have not got the guts but it will be aggressive sin!
Cast this spell on me soon almighty one, for I will be wasted
from this existence and live in a trance of tranquillity!
I will never have that because they have promised
I have tried but I am broken and always will...
It is time on your own accord!

The departed

It's all been a lie and I'm tired…
From the tender swallow
To the split
Why did you lie to me for?
I've been hurt today, yesterday and tomorrow because of this!
This rope hung and shot
This clear blood
These shattered pumps
Don't kill me… but release me from this pornography
I am the departed
My life is a lie!

The glass of barbed wire and you're not alone!

This darkness unburied once again
The demons aloft and fly
This anger cultivates to this black, scratchy and agonizing spot!
Your service to those of who are aware of your good… is not enough!
Bless those with open hugs to the kiss
Those of the unknown and wanted and it will surpass you!
Right now… this time is not my time but I will create out of love…
Under the watchful eye!
Death maybe the only unwanted sin
But be aware of this defeat…
For it will only be victorious by you and me!
You will be broken for too short, to gain this inspiration!
For it will return in mysterious and mystical ways for only you!
This toxic waste only buries the molten lead in your heart but if controlled, with time and patience…
You will experience gold through the cracks!
It will not be like this for always…
For we are the caked vase under, over and wrapped in this barbed wire…
It is only suffocation and breath…!

The truth of being deranged

The truth of the true poet!
A gentle angry soul
A sexual split, maniac of overdose excessive
Not only in this…
Only addiction dead meat in the eyes of god!
Is this were he needs to be, to see this all unfold?
Scrape his arse of the bottom pocket of change!
Needs to be here to downer inspired, of the psychological
nature!
He will be there with you, RIGHT IN NOW…
Never going anywhere and he loves you always!
Bless this tortured soul of a man?
For what he has sown shall reap only in the life after!

There is a caterpillar in my tea!

the dust of being a struggling poet and confused philosopher
is this….

Precaution…
"contents"
There is a caterpillar in my tea1

There is a fact to the point, on the art to my life!

Catalystic change will eventually make me a successful poet
and wise philosopher
But…
I know it's disgusting and it tastes so sweetly with shame!

"little boy"

Come back

Clean and clear is the path
Dirty and disturbed is my contradictory leaks
Creating fully, every second chances we get
Build up from these shattered and broken pieces... of
addictive habits that can be changed...
If INTENTED!
Dream life seems so far sometimes but if implanted... you will
see it all the time progressing!
IT'S A PROCESS...
DON'T GIVE UP...
YOUR NEARLY THERE!
I had it all once before
Five years gone and thought I had been crushed
Now I see it set me on the Eiffel tower, with all the puzzle
pieces to click!
HERE I COME!
Get in the development...
If you die along the road... you will die happy!
To get there, is to give... DON'T FORGET!

Dark nature

Fill this kettle to the brim
These empty cups in a row
Diluted with these leafy sandbags
These holes new, sticky and brown
Though each cup selected for each mouth
The rage of needed
To parch each lip
Not just carelessly wanted
Which brings this man's steel grin to soft
As he talks the cotton candy smiles
Brings him down from the twisted god's clouds and stabilizes
his dark nature!

Don't waste your carnation…

Silky smooth pyjamas and hairy slippers
Caffeinated oily throat from the boil
Layed out on the lazy
No special hits just the masked vigilante
A medicated poem
One whole slice and half a bag
Know he sleeps with such sweet release
Don't waste your carnation!

Faith, forgiveness and forever light

Pounce downtown for my pudding
Coke at last...
My addiction is comforted
As I puff and sniff in life, it is complex yet a simple grasp
I laugh on sedated occasion
Fucked off...
Yet for what I have sown is yet not reaped...
Damn it
Each moment in light I have been screened in pitch and layed
in the ditch
A once guardian knight
From a knower to a doer
Hater of self
Yet loved
A crippled emotional distort
I am the red opaque Buddha that does not have any
judgement and we are the sons and daughters of god in all of
us
Creation of a world together out of love and fascination!

Little Boy

Is this your last cup of tea?

Swamped by this…
Yet the equation was solved by honesty
You cried in my arms of home
Walk out of here but will this be…your last cup of tea?
A heavy burden on your love and head ready to pop
In this long dark narrow road
What could we give back for all that we have learnt?
What have we received from all of this hurt?
Let's find ourselves an escapism that brings around this
peace
If not have a dream
Let's create one and leave all behind us!

Slabs

The perfect pictured night
The souls twinkle and the god moons
The muck has us 3…
The self
The others
The spirit of power and force…!
Either lay more to your destiny and purpose
Though in walk…
The created may simply disintegrate, be broken or pushed to
the side!
You have a start
It's up to you to lay the slabs in control and in out!

The truth of energy

Talk to me?
Sit down?
Cup of tea and a smoke?
Your sexual forest has jealousies me
This paranoia has got the better of me!
My love and anger seeps slowly out of my skin!
Kill me now but wait a moment and cherish it!
You know what...
FUCK YOU... FUCK YOU demonic!
You are not me, myself and I!
You will never control but thank you for the fuel...!
You have made me a server of life
This destroyed boy now a man, will work with the angels and
demons, to create and serve!
So... so... TRUTH!

This fearful war!

You are my predator and my war
This battle we commence…

I wish at times it was physically comfortable
Only at times and out of fear
Mentally revengeful…

I have twisted your neck broke, killed you and bitten your
precious nose off!
Death is too good for you
Years I was a Zen dog
After…

Years I have built and sharpened an armour
Now I want, need and started to bare

I may not like your stand but I love your humanity
Even though there is this beast but there is also love and care
in your walk

As I pick up this concrete… wanting to smash your skull
I lay bareback on the cracked and cold pavement of
surrender!
One more time
Hit me…
Hit me…
FUCKING HIT ME!
For one smack may kill me for my bow
I may die but it is my epiphany!

On this sofa and in this bath…
I have beaten a china-Englishman to purple, black and blue1

I will image my lips kissing your head because that's all I can
achieve in this fearful war…
But my love and time is needed elsewhere!

Through dawn to dust!

Sharp, dedicated and at peace I once was
Now... a soft, blunt and disturbed, is all I brush
I am not that little boy I once talked and wrote about before!
I am a little man that needs to conquer my dark shaky self
From granted to settled!
Be new, with forever future...., kissing and holding hands...
To the dawn to dust!

Through

Electric floodlights on my way
A dampener on the now
I pray for you and me, so we see god on our way
Within and throughout!
Through this chocolate grit
I find a sharpened finesse that I will cherish through my sinew
Defeat these faces with confront and repetitive strain.
If I don't accept they came from this glory hole…
I will never dissolve in!
Don't wait to crash and snap
Cure through control!

# Little Boy